Real Head,
Knees & Elbows

Real Head, Knees & Elbows

Geoff Thompson

SUMMERSDALE

Summersdale Publishers Ltd
46 West Street
Chichester
West Sussex
PO19 1RP
United Kingdom

Photographs by David W Monks
Member of the Master Photographer's Association
Snappy Snaps Portrait Studio
7 Cross Cheaping
Coventry
CV1 1HF

A CIP Catalogue for this book is available from the British
Library.

Printed and bound in Great Britain by Biddles Ltd, Guildford and King's Lynn.

ISBN 1 873475 77 2

About the Author:

Geoff Thompson has to be one of the most recognised and controversial martial arts writers and teachers of this century, with over 20 best-selling books and 20 instructional videos on the contemporary role of martial art to his name. His work is both innovative and thought-provoking. As an ambassador for the martial arts he has appeared on national and international television and radio – for several years as the *BBC Good Morning* self-defence expert – talking about and giving advice on self-protection and related subjects.

He has taught his unique method of self-protection to the police, the Royal Marine commandos, in local government, on Excel Bodyguard training camps and also on the professional circuit. Geoff's first book *Watch My Back – A Bouncer's Story* (released in the USA by Paladin Press) about his nine years working as a nightclub doorman is widely recognised as a cult book. His other books have also been highly successful. He has appeared in numerous publications including: *SG's Martial Arts*, *Combat*, *Traditional Karate*, *Fighters*, *Terry O'Neill's Fighting Arts International*, *Muscle Mag* (Britain – USA), *Black Belt Magazine* (USA) *Fighters* (Sweden) and

Australasian Fighting Arts (Australia). He is currently Sub-Editor of *Martial Arts Illustrated*. He has also featured in mainstream glossy magazines such as *Loaded*, *Maxim* and *Esquire* and has published several articles with *GQ* Magazine (Britain – Paris).

In 1997 Geoff was flown out to the United States by Chuck Norris and Richard Norton to teach his unique method of self-protection on their international martial arts seminar alongside martial art greats: Benny 'the jet' Urquediz and Rigan and Jean-Jacques Machado.

As well as his books and videos Geoff has written a feature film based on his life and 12 television plays based on his bouncer books. Although recognised as an international authority on the art of self-protection, his work in reality and cross training in combat is still thought of as heresy in some quarters of the martial arts world.

Other books and videos by Geoff Thompson:

Watch My Back – A Bouncer's Story
Bouncer (sequel to *Watch My Back*)
On the Door – *Further Bouncer Adventures.*
The Pavement Arena – *Adapting Combat Martial Arts to the Street*
Real Self-defence
Real Grappling
Real Punching
Real Kicking
Dead Or Alive – *Self-protection*
3 Second Fighter – The Sniper Option
Weight Training – For the Martial Artist
Animal Day – Pressure Testing the Martial Arts
Tuxedo Warrior: *Tales of a Mancunian Bouncer,* by Cliff Twemlow,
foreword by Geoff Thompson
Fear – The Friend of Exceptional People: techniques in controlling fear
Blue Blood on the Mat by Athol Oakley, foreword by Geoff Thompson
Give Him To The Angels – *The Story Of Harry Greb* by James R Fair

The Art of Fighting Without Fighting –
Techniques in threat evasion

The Ground Fighting Series (books):
Vol. One   – Pins, the Bedrock
Vol. Two   – Escapes
Vol. Three – Chokes and Strangles
Vol. Four   – Arm Bars and Joint Locks
Vol. Five   – Fighting From Your Back
Vol. Six   – Fighting From Neutral Knees

Videos:
Lessons with Geoff Thompson
Animal Day – Pressure Testing the Martial Arts
Animal Day Part Two – The Fights
Three Second Fighter – The Sniper Option
Throws and Take-Downs Vols. 1-6
Real Punching Vols. 1-3
The Fence

The Ground Fighting Series (videos):
Vol. One   – Pins, the Bedrock
Vol. Two   – Escapes
Vol. Three – Chokes and Strangles
Vol. Four   – Arm Bars and Joint Locks
Vol. Five   – Fighting From Your Back
Vol. Six   – Fighting From Neutral Knees

Advanced Ground Fighting Vols. 1-3

Pavement Arena Part 1

Pavement Arena Part 2

     – The Protection Pyramid

Pavement Arena Part 3

     – Grappling, The Last Resort

Pavement Arena Part 4

     – Fit To Fight

Contents

Foreword by Dave Turton   15

Introduction   23

Chapter One: The Head   29

Chapter Two: Knees   47

Chapter Three: Elbows   69

Conclusion   96

Foreword

by Dave Turton
6th Dan

When Geoff asked me to write a foreword to his latest work not only was I delighted as always to help a close friend, but also, it made me think strongly about what I wanted to say on the subject of head, knees and elbows.

As I am sure you will be aware, Geoff is heavily into the practical side of martial art, and any method of combat that involves reality will be close to his heart. So you can be sure that Geoff is the right man to guide you through the do's and don'ts of working with these close-range weapons. Therefore reading this text (if you follow the advice given) will be well worth the effort.

I have been involved with the real side of combat for more years than I care to remember. And in all my time the 3 weapons Geoff is describing herein, were not only a strong part of my main artillery, they were often the only options I had in real fights.

Real Head, Knees & Elbows

From the very beginning I was taught how useful these weapons are, and drilled long and hard on their uses, and the more I became involved in real and often very violent situations on the doors, the more I gave respect to them.

Treat these techniques with the respect they deserve, work hard on both their technical aspects, and their applications, and I know you will be well rewarded should you ever need to call on their service in a real fight.

A few anecdotes may serve to illustrate just why I believe that knees, elbows and heads are more than just support techniques!

The first time I witnessed the effectiveness of the close-in work was as an attacker on a 1st Dan grading in Wales, at the headquarters of the Goshinkwai. I was 3rd Kyu at the time, and tried to come in low and sneaky to the right hand side of the would-be black Belt taking on multiple attackers as a part of his grading . . . I was rewarded with a beautiful inward vertical elbow strike to my left ear. I saw more stars than Patrick Moore as I dropped down onto one knee. Still dazed and listening to what sounded like a chorus in my head, I was rudely awakened with a left knee to the other side of my head. At this point I lost all interest in the grading and can vouch first hand for the effectiveness of elbows and knees.

Coming round (moments later) at the side of the mat I realised, thanks to the rather rough lesson I had just been given, that with the right range and angle, knee and elbow attacks are devastating.

The originator of our system, the Late Great Kenshiro Abbe, was a firm believer in close range combat, specifically head, knees and elbows . . . often when using a Judo-style grip on an opponent in a Gi, Abbe would whip in a knee to the outside of the thigh prior to a throw, or perform two or even three fast headbutts to weaken the opponent for throwing.

On the floor Abbe rarely used any other strikes other than elbows and head to set up his adversary for a punishing hold.

We often practised the elbow as a long range attacking move: just trying to elbow could psyche the opponent out.

The elbow is one of the few weapons that are not limited by the angle you are to your opponent . . . whether he is at your side, rear or in front, there is an elbow strike that will fit the scenario.

In the seventies we were treated to the arrival of three top Thai Boxers, namely Woody, Toddy and Ken, as they were affectionately known. The Thais have taken the art of knees and elbows to a level most of us would be thrilled to reach . . . I saw just how good late in 1979 at a club in Oldham called the Cats Whiskers. I was on the door, and so was Ken (Master Sken) . . . during my routine walk about the inside of the club, I heard a commotion at the front door. We had been visited by several Maoris from a touring rugby team: the smallest was about 16 stones. By the time I had crossed the floor Ken had taken four of them to KO using only knees and elbows. I was astonished at the sheer power of these moves. I arrived just in time to see the last one hit the deck. Ken hit him in the head with a hooking elbow, grabbed him around the head with both hands and then followed immediately with a jumping knee to the head of the Maori who fell unconscious with his three friends. My only involvement was in helping to drag the victims away from the door.

On another occasion, at a less than salubrious establishment in Rochdale known as the Lamplighter (the Lamplighter's motto was 'have a laugh at the Lamplighter or cause trouble . . . either way you go home in stitches'). I was attempting to walk a would-be troublemaker to the doors when, as I found out later, his big (I mean Big) brother took exception to the fact and lifted me about 9 inches off the floor. Thanks to my training, I managed three fast rear headbutts, and when he let go of my arms to protect his face I followed with a rear right elbow to his right ear. When he dropped to the floor I finished with a left rear elbow to the pubes . . . the only really hard work was dragging him off the premises.

You might be surprised to know that the head is used as a weapon tool in most cultures around the world, indeed the Eskimos, because of the amount of protective clothing they had to wear to fight off the cold, often used close grips and headbutts as their main artillery. The (African) Capoeira champions have several headbutts in their system, as do the Bantu tribe. These are mainly wrestlers who use the 'head' as a means of releasing holds. They all practise on impact equipment. However, if you decide to do likewise, practise slowly at first: the head must be 'set' and 'formed' and not 'upset' and 'deformed'.

Getting back to the book, I know Geoff is well versed in using all these methods in real situations . . . so much so, in fact, I have often thought that Geoff hit with his head because it was his least vulnerable weapon. What do they say, where there is no sense there is no feeling? But I have to say this isn't true (after all I am training with him this weekend). No, Geoff uses his head in many ways in real situations and using the head as a weapon is a method well worth the effort.

Power is generated inside the body mainly from the waist, hips and legs working with muscular contractions to produce internal energy ready for transmission to the limbs. As with perfecting most things in life, the reality is repetition and what is repetition if it isn't boring? And no one can accuse these close-range attacks of being 'flashy' or 'showy' . . . but if you want to make them workable then repetition and 'boring' is where it is at. These techniques *need* to be 'drilled'. They need to be practised from the correct distances and from multiple angles. They need to be practised in both vertical and horizontal positions. They also need to be worked on the heavy bag for power development. Often the sheer hard work needed to make these weapons useful in a real scenario is their downfall because whilst these techniques do work, most students do not.

Read this book; it will show you how to train head, knees and elbows to their best effect, and you're getting the advice from one of the world's foremost combat authors and practitioners.

Head, knees and elbows are weapons *par excellence*, but reading this book will only make you aware of them – following the invaluable advice of its author is what will take them from paper to pavement.

Happy reading.

Dave Turton
6th Dan Goshinkwai Combat

Introduction

Welcome to *Real Head, Knees and Elbows*, at long last. I have been threatening to write this book for, oh, I don't know how long – apologies for its delay.

This is the last in the *Real Series* and, basically I have written it to tie up the loose ends from the other *Real* books. Not that this text is any less important than the others – far from it – a chain is only as strong as its weakest link. It has to be said that I do consider the techniques herein to be a part, a very valuable part, of the support system. I always consider 'hands' to be the main artillery and the most effective weapon in the race for good, physical self-protection. This is primarily because punching range is the one most given in a live scenario. This is just my opinion however, I have many friends, as will be evident throughout the text, who employ either head knees or elbows as a main artillery technique and very effectively I have to say. I use them as a support system to back my hands should they let me down or should the situation not favour that range.

Real Head, Knees & Elbows

Neither head, knee or elbow techniques will work for you unless you master them, unless you make them your own. I have used all three successfully in real situations, on several occasions. However I have to be honest also and say that, as a younger man still struggling with real violence I have also used all three unsuccessfully. Only good luck and/or providence pulled me through when the techniques, or rather my poor execution of them, fell apart like a cheap suit. My head butts were badly aimed and I nearly knocked myself out of two occasions, my knees were slow, predictable and pushy and did little more than expend energy that was vitally needed in other areas of the fight and my elbows just couldn't find the right range. It was with my dismal failures in mind that I took to perfecting these potentially devastating techniques making them explosive, accurate and economical, and also using them when the range was favourable as opposed to just blasting them out willy-nilly.

I was in a good position 'on the door' because people were constantly picking fights with me. Seemingly (to the uninitiated) the weakest member of a hard door, I had ample opportunity to try lots of different techniques to see what worked and what did not and to perfect the techniques that I felt had potential. I know that this might sound like a very violent statement, I also realise that in this period of my life I was a very violent man. However, I believe that whether I was right or wrong to get into so many fights, you still want to learn from my experience. What is also worth remembering, is the fact that although I used these situations to practice my technique, they were unsolicited attacks upon me. I never looked for trouble and all of those potential opponents that allowed me to talk them down, walked away without a bashing. Those that got a bashing were those that wanted to fight with me for whatever reason. So I perfected my techniques in the field.

I think I should also underline at this point in the book that just because I favour hands in the live scenario does not mean anything other than, 'I favour hand techniques'. You, like some of my friends may not favour hands. If that is the case try to tailor these concepts to fit your favoured main artillery. Don't become a clone of Geoff Thompson or Joe Bloggs or John Doe or whoever. If the concepts are sound, which in this, and all my texts, they surely are, then mould your technique around these concepts. Don't imitate, innovate.

Try to work around the contemporary enemy and environment, that is, don't try and throw a kick a punch a knee and elbow etc, if the range is wrong. Work with the energy and dimensions that the situation gives you. One of the reasons that I use these techniques as a support rather than main artillery is the very close proximity that they demand if they are going to work. I generally use head, knees and elbows when I have been grabbed, using the opponent's clothing as leverage. And even then I tend to use them in combination to finish an opponent. Very rarely will one of these techniques singularly finish the opponent.

As I said before, and forgive me for repeating myself, some of my friends have made these techniques their own and do attack with them outside of vertical grappling range. People like Master Sken, the legendary Thai boxer, has had tremendous success with knees and elbows in real situations. Fighters like Tony Roberts very rarely used anything other than his head and could, from any range, demolish whole teams with his butting ability. Although they are very much specialist, they do serve to demonstrate the awesome potential of the head, knees and elbows. These latter techniques fill the, often large, gaps in the fighting artillery, between punching, kicking and grappling, they help to complete the circle as it were. The techniques in this book, like all techniques really (and like all things in life) need constant maintenance or they will atrophy.

Chapter One

The Head

'Tony had to be carrying 22 stone over a 6 foot frame with a large belly at the front and legs like tree trunks. His face was also big, but as charismatic as they come, with scars running this way and that through his cheeks and eyebrows from several stabbings in some of the worst shit holes this side of 1920s Shanghai. He'd been stabbed by brothers, sisters, mothers and fathers in his time on the door. If we are talking about being stabbed Tony is the metaphoric pin-cushion. Once, when restraining a youth in a nightclub in the centre of town, he felt a sharp pain under his right armpit. He thought little more of it until he let the lad go and dropped his arm only to find a stiletto blade sticking out of his ribs. 'I don't remember leaving that there?!' he said to his side kick before collapsing on the floor.

Another time he opened the doors of a nightclub, now closed down because of the heavy volume of gratuitous violence, to be faced with a mad axe man, already in full swing with a rusty, heavy wood chopping axe. Sure that this was to be his *coup de grace*, because there was no way he could stop the axe from finding a bed in his skull, Tony closed his eyes and awaited the most dreaded finale. It never came. Only a heavy thud above his head. He carefully opened one eye and then the other only to discover that the axe had been swung so high and so hard that it had hit the top frame of the door and stuck fast. The wielder was swinging off the axe to try and release it so that he could 'try again'. It turned out to be a guy that he'd thrown out earlier in the night. He desperately tugged and pulled at the axe in an attempt to free it.

Tony, not one to miss such a golden opportunity, hit him with a head butt that separated him from the axe – and the ground – and sent him sprawling into the road like he'd been shot from a cannon. He lay, unconscious, in a bloody heap. The damage was so substantial that the ambulance driver later said he thought the guy had been the victim of a hit and run car accident. The axe man lay motionless for the best part of twenty minutes before the ambulance actually came and scraped up his remains and took him off to hospital. They couldn't straighten his nose, said it looked as though it had been put through a blender.

As you have probably noticed Tony was a 'head' man. And a master thereof. He could head butt with missile accuracy from as far away as six foot and as close as whispering in your ear. I never saw any one survive the mighty wrath of a Tony R head butt. He also taught me to use the head and though it is not my main artillery technique it is a favoured strike. I tend to use it spontaneously – ask any of my sparring partners – if the situation gives me the right openings.'

Extract from *On The Door*

The head has to be one of the most effective techniques available, if used correctly. If used incorrectly the head can be as dangerous to the attacker, as to the recipient. Surprisingly very few people ever fully get to grips with this devastating phenomenon. Many feel that they are going to hurt their own head should they use it as an attacking tool to the face of an assailant. This is sad really because, as Tony 'the head' once said to me, if you hands are tied up the head is another hand. This technique could also be used by women if they had a mind to include it in their curriculum. Again, they disallow it from their training because they feel that butting someone in the face is not very lady-like. That's exactly why they should use it. No man is every going to expect a women to butt them in the face simply because 'it's not lady-like'. The truth is though, no effective technique is lady-like, they are all ugly, at least the effective ones anyway.

But that's the price you pay if you don't want to be raped up an ally by some low life who has decided to step outside the law to satisfy his lustful urges. If you are talking about real encounters, the blood and snot type that occur on our streets every single day of the week, then nothing effective should be disqualified from your artillery.

I remember talking on a seminar of instructors once, and I happened to mention that biting was an excellent technique to use if you were in the shit. One or two of the instructors shot me disapproving glances, one even shook his head and 'tutted'. They said that they couldn't bite another person, yet when I watched them training the were practising knife hand attacks to the throat, finger strikes to the eyes etc – maybe someone can explain to me the difference here. How is whacking someone in the throat, a killing technique, any better, or any more wholesome than biting someone. Generally a bite is a superfluous attack in that, although painful to the recipient, it is rarely life threatening. It might leave an ugly scar but it is unlikely to blind them, like an eye attack, or kill them, like a throat attack. Wake up please.

Only recently, on the national news there was a report of a man killed outside his local fish and chip shop after a 'minor' argument with some men in the shop. I wonder whether they, or any of the attackers out there, are worried about what they attack innocents with. Somehow I think not!

The key factor in the success of the head butt is to keep your attack below the opponent's eye line. Anywhere above is potentially dangerous to the bestower. Paradoxically you, the person employing the butt, must use only that which is above the eye line as an attacking tool, or again you may end up with as many injuries as your opponent. You can attack effectively with the head in any one of five different ways:

1)   From left to right, using the right corner of your forehead to attack

2)   From right to left, using the left corner of your forehead to attack

3)   A forward thrusting head butt using the left, centre or right corner of your forehead to attack

4) Attack upward with the crown of your head

5) Attack backward with the back of your head

The butt you choose will vary according to the circumstances in which you find yourself and the technique that you favour. They are all close range techniques that can be employed with or without the support of an opponent's clothing. Power in the butt relies upon two major things. Firstly, the whiplashing effect of your head as you lurch forward to attack – the body weight being projected slightly before the head, secondly the momentum of the propelling body weight (which should still be travelling forward as the head strikes its target), adding weight and travel to the said attack.

Left to right:

Please try to follow the pictures here, they will show the technique better than a description. It goes without saying that I would ask a question before attacking, so as to engage the opponent's brain, thus ensuring a window of entry. Lurch your body forward followed by your head. The left corner of your forehead should follow the body weight travel and whiplash into the opponent's face or jaw. If you are actually in a vertical embrace and have a grip of the opponent's clothing at the time of your attack then pull them, via their attire rapidly toward the butt.

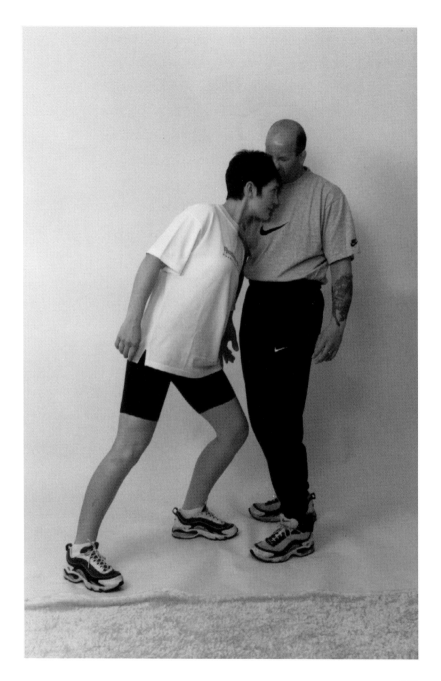

Right to left:

Exactly the same here, only you are attacking from right to left, as opposed to from left to right. Lurch your body forward followed by your head. The right corner of your forehead should follow the body weight travel and whiplash into the opponent's face or jaw. If you are actually in a vertical embrace and have a grip of the opponent's clothing at the time of your attack then pull them, via the attire rapidly toward the butt.

Forward thrusting head butt:

Lurch your body directly forward followed by the front of your forehead (or either side of the head if you prefer), whiplashing it into the opponent's face or jaw. Care should be taken when attacking from the front not to hit the opponent's teeth. Although your attack will do the damage you will also incur injury. I know of many fighters that have received terrible injuries from hitting the teeth of an adversary. I myself spent a week in hospital to remove an abscess from the knuckles of my right hand after punching an adversary in the teeth. So beware, the teeth are a no no.

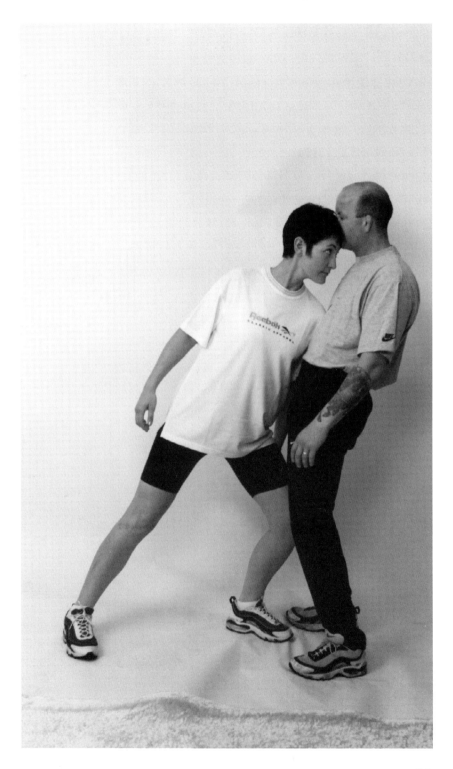

Upward head butt:

Generally this attack is employed from within vertical grappling range, when your forehead is in the region of the opponent's chest, as per illustration – or anywhere below his chin. From this position thrust the head upward as rapidly as you can, attacking the opponent's chin with the front crown of your own head. Drive right through for maximum effect.

'I didn't do anything at first, except try to get up. As I did our heads clashed. The back of mine with the front of his. I felt the weight lift off my back as he rolled over and groaned. I don't think I've ever moved so fast in all my life. I was up and away down the tow path like a shot.'
Extract from *Unleash the Lioness*.

As you can see from this extract, the head can be devastating and effective, even when used by accident. This woman, in the midst of an attempted rape scenario felled her attacker by accident with a devastating reverse head butt.

Reverse head butt:

This attack is potentially one of the most dangerous head attacks because of the pure surprise of it. Of course, like all things, it needs much practice for it to be instinctive. This attack is only useful when your opponent is directly behind you. Either grabbing you or preparing to grab you. If you have not been grabbed but the attacker is about to grab you then use your body weight in the attack by lurching backwards, whiplashing the back of your head into the face of the opponent.

If the attacker has you in a bear hug type scenario, there for neutralising your body weight bring your head slightly forward and lash it back,

Real Head, Knees & Elbows

hard and as many time as it takes to release his grip, into his face.

Whenever it is possible I always bend at the knee when I butt, so that I can explode the attack into the target. Also by bending at the knee I lower myself below the opponent's eye-line, taking away the danger of hitting my head on his head – something that I have done twice and do not wish to do again.

For the record I have seen many demonstrations, via book and video where one person attacks the other by butting him in the forehead. Please don't ever do this. In theory it should work, in practice is certainly does not. You are as likely to knock yourself out as you are your attacker. Listen to a man that has done it for real, the right way and the wrong way.
The head is also very effective on the floor, for example, when you are ground fighting with an opponent. Especially from what is commonly called the 'mount position'.

Head butting from the mount:
When I attack from here it is usually multiple attacks, my intention being to knock the opponent out or force him over onto his belly so that I can choke him out. Please follow the illustrations below for a better look at how it works.

Real Head, Knees & Elbows

To open the facial target up (the opponent will protect his face in this scenario at all costs), I will usually strike first with my fists. As soon as the opponent's guard is taken away I will drive forward with multiple butts until he is out or he turns to protect his face. If he turns I will wrap my right (or left) arm around his throat to secure the choke (or strangle).

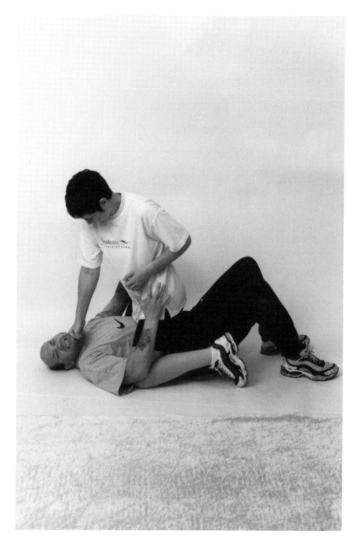

Chapter Two

Knees

'Bob and his partner, a comedy duo, were playing the student gig at one of their regular venues. This was a part time thing for Bob, whose full time occupation was as a martial arts instructor, his main style being that of Muay Thai. The act was going down well and the crowd seemed to appreciate the raucous humour that the two attacked them with. Part of the act involved insulting, in the best possible taste of course, members of the audience. It was never taken badly (not until tonight least ways), and was usually accepted in the vein that it was delivered. Occasionally a heckler, a would-be stand up, would aim the odd verbal missile only to be shot down in flames by these two brilliant professionals.

Bob had noticed the staring Neanderthal standing at the side of the stage attacking him and his partner with looks that could kill. He took no notice initially after all, the act was X-rated, and not everyone found it to their taste.

Real Head, Knees & Elbows

As the act went on, the stare from the side stage mammalian got stronger and he edged closer and closer to the stage. His arms were starting to splay, like he was carrying rolls of carpet under them and his eyes took on a stare that was conducive with an animal stalking its prey. Bob sensed that the guy was preparing to attack and so tried to catch the eye of one of the bouncers – none were within view. As he continued his act and simultaneously tried to catch the eye of a doorman the man with the stare suddenly exploded onto the stage and raced at him 'arms-a-flailing' like a man possessed. Instinctively Bob grabbed his attacker as he lurched forward and drove a Thai knee deep into his solar plexus – like only a Thai man can – and dropped his adversity like a sack of shit. The crowd gave a murmur of applause and a few giggled supposing that it was all a part of the show (it was that kind act!). A bouncer appeared from the door and dragged what was left of the guy out of the club and left him, still gasping for breath, in the cold night air.

Bob and his partner continued their act concluding with Bob chopping a melon in half, across an audience member's bared stomach, with a Samurai sword no less. I can only conclude by saying that I'm only glad that the fella didn't attack during this part of the act, otherwise there would have been more than melon being severed on stage with a four foot sword.'

The knees of course, were made legendary by the great Muay Thai boxers, such as Master Sken, Master Toddy, Master Woody and the effervescent Sandy Holt. They use kneeing techniques as naturally and effectively as the western boxer uses his hands. I would say that 'the knees' are relegated to in-fighting or grappling range though irreplaceable when the range is right.

Again the specialist, some of those mentioned above as a for instance, will, can and do use the knees from all ranges inside and outside of grappling range, and to great effect. But they are masters of the knee and elbow and so are exceptions to the rule. If you wish to specialise in any given technique you too can break the rules.

The knees may be used effectively to attack upward, forward, roundways, inwards, jumping or, to a felled opponent, as a finishing technique downward. Attacking as low as the opponent's knee or as high as his head. The attacks are very accessible, very basic and in some case demand only a low skill factor. This is very important if it is going to work for a person, a recreational player, that does not want to dedicate his whole life to training.

Upward Knee

This is the basic upward knee technique that you see on all self-defence programmes where the women teacher says, like she's talking about a recipe or something, 'just knee him in the testicles for the desired results.' That's not to say of course that this is not an effective technique, it really is. However, no attack, not even with a gun, holds a guarantee to drop the opponent dead.

As stated the problem with kneeing techniques is that you generally have to be close to an opponent. This means close enough for him to grab you and drag you to the floor – not the best place to be in a violent encounter, especially when facing multiple opponents or indeed one determined opponent that wants you on the floor in the first place. I get sick of seeing kneeing techniques as the flag-ship of so many hypothetical self-defence productions which intimate that this technique will guarantee to finish an encounter should it be employed – not so. No technique holds such a guarantee, and to believe that they do, is to ill prepare yourself for an arena that is ferocious and ugly.

My first couple of attempts at kneeing techniques, in real encounters failed abysmally because my attacks were clumsy and pushy. This was not helped by the fact that I was wearing trousers that stuck to my thighs as I tried to lift my knee. In theory and in perfect conditions it should be easy to generate power with the knee, in reality with adrenal shake in the legs and constrictive clothing it is far from easy. For a knee attack to work it needs to be sharp and explosive, this means much practice. A slow technique not only lacks power, it is also easy for an aggressor to catch. If he grabs your leg you are as good as on the ground and if that's where he wanted you in the first place then you are in a world of trouble, as they say. I'll talk in a moment about the different attacks you can employ with the knee.

The knee attack is best aimed at the groin or testicles, or if for some reason the opponent is bent over, the face. You could pull the opponent over so that the face is more accessible, but from my experience, opponents don't just let you 'pull them over' and will resist like their very life depends upon it (it may well do). So rather aim for targets that are readily available.

Lift the knee upward as sharply as possible. A slow pushy movement would probably be ineffective, the quicker the ascent, the greater the impact. If applying the same technique to the opponent's head or face, first grab his head by the hair or ears or by coupling your hands up at the back of his head and pull his head down rapidly as you thrust your knee into his face. As they meet smash your knee through his face.

As I said earlier, if you have the choice better to go for the lower extremities than try to knee him in the head by dragging his head to your knee. His wedding tackle is already there waiting to be attacked so why travel anywhere else when it is not necessary. If however you attempt to attack the groin and he bends over to thwart your strike, then he has presented his head for attack, on the platter as it were. Go with the energy, take what he gives you.

Forward Knee:

I must admit that this is my most favoured kneeing technique, though the skill factor is higher due to the fact that you have to incorporate more hip extension. But the results are worth the training. If you connect properly with this technique it is devastating and effective.

This technique is much the same as the thrusting front kick using the knee as the attacking tool as opposed to the foot. It relies heavily on the grip you have on the opponent, though I have to repeat, the better Thai fighters will successfully employ all these techniques with or without the leverage of an opponent's clothing. Grab the opponent's attire tightly at about shoulder level and vigorously push him away from you, this will force him into an equal and opposite reaction, that is he will push back, as he does steal the energy that he gives you and pull viciously. Simultaneously, thrust the attacking knee upward and forward to meet the opponent's body on its descent. At the moment of impact thrust both hips forward and into the opponent's body whilst still pulling downward with the grip. This is probably the best one, but the hardest to perfect because you need to perfect so many elements, not least the flow, going with the opponent's energy.

Roundhouse knee:

I like the roundhouse knee, though I have to say that it is not, in my opinion, a stopping technique. It is good though to create openings and at the very least weaken an opponent. The skill factor here is high again, so vigilant practice is needed.

The roundhouse knee is much the same as the roundhouse kick, using the knee as the attacking tool as opposed to the foot. It, also, is relegated to grappling distance and relies much on the pulling/grabbing support of an opponent's clothing. Maybe used very effectively to attack the opponent's knee or thigh. Sometimes you can attack the body but there is a danger of the leg getting caught mid strike and you being forced over. Advanced fighters do this technique to the head of an opponent, literally turning it into a flying knee attack. I wouldn't recommend this unless you are highly skilled.

To the knee, thigh or body lift the attacking knee up and slightly away from your body then thrust it downward toward the target and at the same time pulling the opponent via his attire toward the attacking knee. On impact thrust your hips forward and slightly drop your body weight into the technique.

Inward Knee attack:

I have listed this technique here though, I have to say that I don't find it that effective. I think it can help to wear an opponent down in a contest but that is hardly what we are looking at here. Even the better fighters haven't inspired me with this technique, though I am sure that there are those out there that can make it work. Me, I find that the energy used in employing it far out ways any result you get from the attack.

Pick the knee off the floor and, using the inside of the knee, attack the opponent's thigh or side, as per illustration.

Jumping front Knee:

This is one of those techniques that looks over-flashy and benign, until you try it on someone, then it turns into a bone smashing technique that stops opponents like an axe across the knee. When I first started practising this move, hitting the pads etc. I felt that the effort to jump and knee was not worth the little power you seemed to deliver on the other end. I didn't realise at the time that the pads were not the right equipment to practice this attack on, in fact I couldn't find anything, other than a partner in training, to practice on that allowed me to see, more specifically feel, the potential of this technique. It's similar in this respect to a head butt. If you demonstrate a head butt on the bag or pad or strike shield it looks and feels weak and pushy, and yet when you apply the same technique to an opponent it is devastating. My first realisation of this, with the jumping knee, was when I tried it out in full contact sparring. The first person I tried it on dropped like a sack of shit with his face a mass of blood, I hadn't even put it in that hard, just the momentum and the impact of bone on face was enough to do the damage. Subsequently everyone that I practised my new-found technique on ended up on the bench nursing a sore and bleeding head. Note: I think that I need to say at this point that the people I train with are all hardened fighters and all our training is to knock out or submission, I would hate anyone to think that I would take advantage of lesser fighters to perfect my technique. I always took it as well as I gave it.

Back to the technique. As I said the likes of Master Sken do use this technique without the aid of grappling leverage, this is a very advanced and athletic endeavour. Personally I use it inside vertical grappling and always use the opponent as leverage for my strike, as you will see clearly by the illustrations.

When the distance falls from kicking/punching to vertical grappling I always try and secure a grip around the back of the opponent's neck with my right or left hand, preferably right. I pull his head slightly forward so that his face is to the floor. From here I literally hop off my left leg and drive my right knee into the opponent's face, once or multiple attacks if they are offered. Simultaneously I pull his head into my knee to add force to the strike.

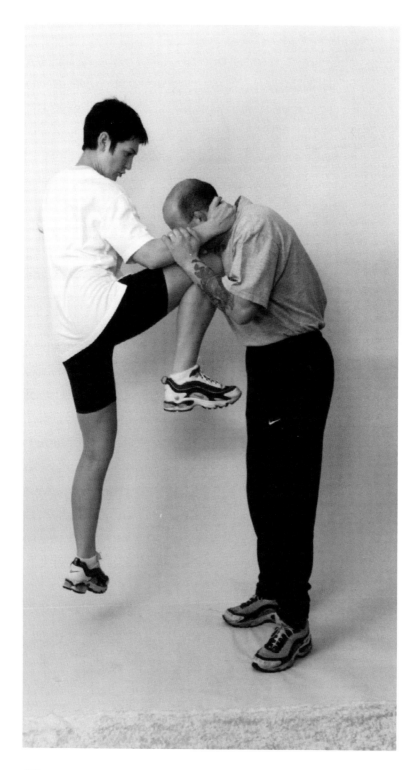

Knee drop:

This is a Garry Spiers speciality, and he does it like no one else. It is a hugely damaging technique that is used to finish off an opponent who is already lying of the floor. Logically, the heavier you are the more effective this technique will be, although it doesn't rely entirely on body weight for its effectiveness. But beware, it can be dangerous for the person attempting the knee drop, due to the danger of him/her being pulled into grappling range by the person on the floor if the technique does not do its job.

Literally, you drop all of your weight forward and down onto the opponent, landing on the target area; ribs, head, etc, with the point of your attacking knee, (left or right). The quicker the descent, the more effective the technique. For added effect you may jump up so that you are landing on the opponent from a greater height.

The danger here is obvious. If the opponent is not finished by your attack he will probably grab you as you drop and you could easily fall in to ground fighting and be beaten by a stronger more experienced person. As a point of fact I do not generally recommend the use of finishing techniques in self-defence, unless the assailant is still a danger to you. Always try to hit and run.

Real Head, Knees & Elbows

Not forgetting though that self-defence and fighting are different and the rules alter according to which arena you enter, or are training for. With self-defence I recommend, on the physical plain, hit and run – no more, no less. In street fighting you would not hit and run, rather you would take the fight to a conclusion, you finish him or he finishes you. If you were working as a doorman the rules are slightly different again, and far too complicated to go into in this text (read *Watch My Back*, *Bouncer* or *On The Door* for more on this).

It is popular, I know, for self-defence teachers to recommend a second and third strike to an attacker who is already stunned. Forget it. Don't even think about it. Anyone that has actually been involved in a real situation would not, or certainly should not, recommend this. If one attack stuns an assailant then use the two or three seconds that this creates to make good your escape. Unless you are highly skilled a stunned, even a semi-conscious assailant will instinctively grab you when you move in for the kill. Then you could have real problems: your attacker is not only hurt, he is pissed off too. I know of many people in self-defence situations who have been beaten to a pulp because they have gone for the *coup de grace* and been grabbed when they should have been a hundred yards away and to safety.

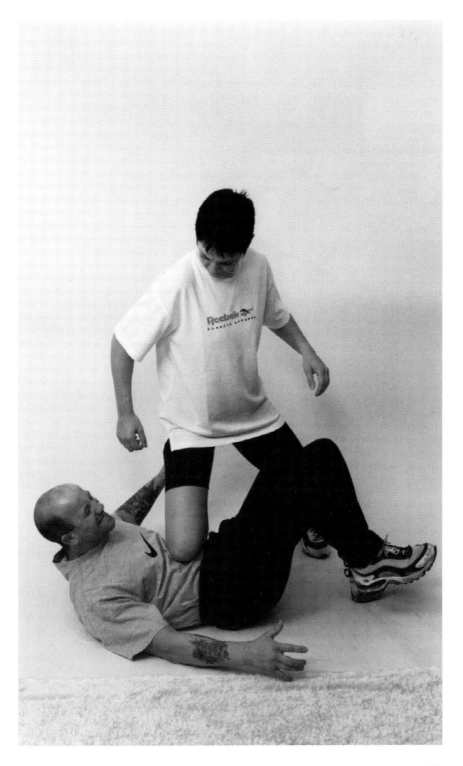

Real Head, Knees & Elbows

The best way to practice knee attacks (although, as I stated the equipment does not always give you an accurate reading of an attack's potential) is on a punch bag. For best effect clothe it, either by tying a loose sack around it or dressing it in old clothes, so that you can grip it like you would a real opponent. Then grab and knee as you would a real person. You may also, if you wish, swing the bag and knee it as it swings toward you. If you lie the bag down on the floor you can practice the knee drop on it. A 6foot bag is great for practising lower region strikes.

You can also use the focus pads, but they are not as effective as the bag. The uke (partner) holds one pad tightly against his thigh with the target area pointing outward whilst at the same time thrusting his knee, (roundhouse), into the pad. To practice the upward knee, the holder should put both hands, (padded) in front of himself at about groin height, right hand overlapping left with both palms facing toward the floor. The attacker may grip the pad holder's hands and pull them downward into the uprising knee or alternatively, grab his attire at shoulder level and pull on them as he executes the knee attack on the pads.

The best way to develop the kneeing techniques is with a partner. If you are looking for a system that use the knee to great effect, or the elbow for that matter, then you need go no further than Thai boxing. In my opinion, they're the real masters when it comes to these deadly attacking tools.

Chapter Three

Elbows

Mick was getting tired. It was 1.30 am, near the end of his shift as a doorman in probably the biggest, busiest nightclub in the centre of town. He had already done a full days work on the sites as a hod carrier. At this moment in time all he could think about was crawling into bed and wrapping his arms around the warm silky body of his lady. Everyone was always telling him what a great job he had, 'an easy number'.

At this moment in time he would rather have been anywhere in the world. Anywhere other than this shit hole where the cigarette smoke attacked his lungs, the music attacked his ears and the woman in front of him, the ugliest thing he had ever seen with only one head, was trying to scratch his eyes out. He kept his fence in front of his face, to parry her hands as they reached for his eyes, and tried unsuccessfully to stop the embarrassed giggle that kept coming from his mouth.

Real Head, Knees & Elbows

The woman was a menace. She'd been caught smoking a joint in the club, against the rules of this establishment, and he had asked he to leave. She had seemed OK at first but now, in the foyer of the club, she had suddenly decided that she was not going to go, not under any circumstances. Mick was left with the unwelcome task of either talking her out or, should the worse come to the worse dragging her out by the panty hose. So undignified, so unnecessary but, the way she was working her mouth and exercising her claws so inevitable.

'Look you bag of sick,' Mick had a nice way with the women, 'you either leave of your own accord or I'll have to physically drag you out. 'S your choice!'

'You touch me and my boyfriend's gonna spark you,' she spat back vehemently.

Mick sighed, the kind that he had sighed so very often when women had threatened him with their men. He knew that this probably meant some poor bloke was going to get a slap trying to prove his manhood.

'I'll give you one more chance to leave. If you don't walk out I'll throw you out.'

The woman dropped her eyebrows and scrunched up her face defiantly. She folded her arms demonstrating that she was not going to be moved. Mick spoke no more and grabbed her and started moving her to the door. From out of nowhere a hunter-gatherer came hurtling towards Mick with a Pils bottle in his hand and bad intention on his mind. It was the boyfriend.

'YAAAAA! Get your ****ing hands of my woman you bast...'

BANG!!

A split second before the bottle landed on Mick's head he released the girl and reverse elbowed the boyfriend straight across the front of his face. It exploded on impact and everyone in the small foyer, including the pot-smoking girlfriend let out a pained 'Ohhhh!' in unison as the bottle wielding mammalian fell to the floor like a dead thing. The girl shut her mouth for the first time all night and looked gobsmacked by the felling of her saviour. Mick also looked down at the sleeping man and thought, not for the first time this week, or this night for that matter, 'so undignified, so unnecessary and yet so inevitable.'

When the time and the distancing are right the elbows can be almost as versatile as the hands, though employed, usually from a shorter range. Many of the trained fighters that I know see the elbows as being *the* main artillery in a real fight, because of the awesome power they can bring to a fight on the punch bag. However, for those that do not know it, the punch bag is a far cry from the street, and whilst it can prepare a fighter for some of the physical elements of a live encounter it in itself is not a 'live' situation. As I said before about the knee and head techniques, you may use them on the pads and feel, because the power does not transmit on that particular piece of equipment, that they are worthless for a real fight. As we have already established this is not the case. The equal and opposite of this is also true, when a technique is awesome on a piece of training equipment, the elbows for instance, the trainee automatically feels that it will be exactly the same outside. From my experience it is not.

A lot of my Thai fighter friends will say to me, 'Oh yeah, but we've got our elbows!' As though being able to elbow correctly is going to turn everything around. Well it won't, let me tell you. And it is not because I don't rate elbow techniques, I do, nor because I don't rate Thai, I do – very highly – I'm an instructor in Thai myself. What I've learned and what I know from being involved in thousands of live fighting scenarios is this: elbowing range, the range between punching and vertical grappling, disappears almost as quickly as it appears. That's the nature of a real fight. So although elbowing techniques are awesome in power and speed, the range that you need to fire them is almost non existent.

I know that there are people out there now who have probably used elbows to effect, I have, some of my friends have, but only when the range was spontaneously right for the technique. The rest of the time you are either punching or grappling. Watch a Thai boxing match and see how many times they elbow through out the fight – very few. That's because the range is a fleeting one that disappears like mist in the middle of a fighting scenario. And the Thais are the masters of this technique.

When the range and the energy are right though, the elbows are awesome. That's why they are included in this text (and also because a book called *Real Head, Knees and Elbows* would look pretty odd without any elbow techniques). So my advice is learn these techniques, develop them even master them, but don't expect too much from them because the range of a real fight rarely favours the elbows. Due to the close proximity of the elbow to the body they are, potentially, more powerful than the hands, however, they lack the 'feel', accuracy and cunning of the hands.

Downward strike
(against a waist or leg grab):

Lift your right (or left) arm up high with the palm of your hand facing away from you. Pull it down in a rapid descent aiming the point of the elbow at and into the target, (spine, neck, rib cage).

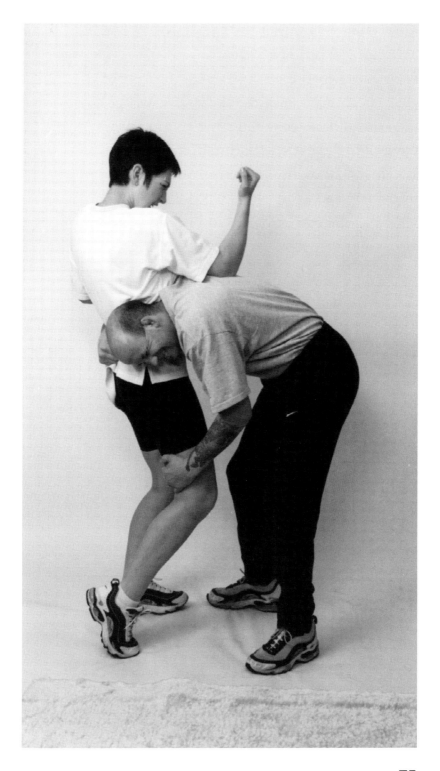

Side thrust (against an assailant attacking from the side):

Bring your right (or left) arm across the front of your chest, palm inwards, as far as it will go, then thrust back along the same route, aiming the point of the elbow into the oncoming or stationary attacker. Target the Solar Plexus, throat or face.

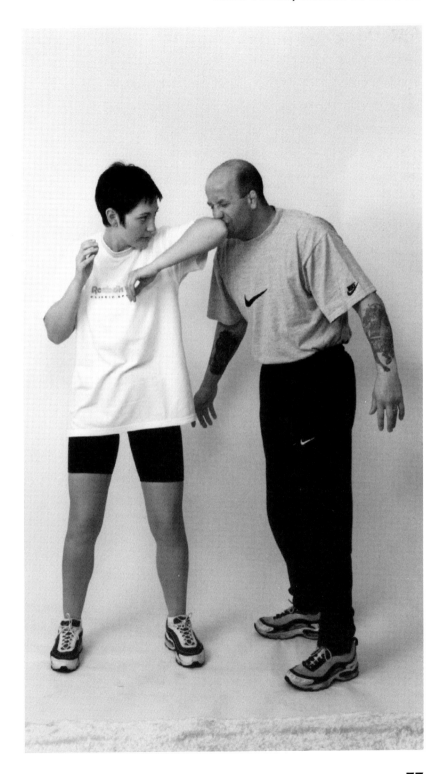

Real Head, Knees & Elbows

Reverse elbow:

Stretch your right arm out in front of you. Turn you head and look at the target behind. Sharply retract your arm back from its out-stretched position and behind you, aiming the point of your elbow at and into the assailant, simultaneously, step back with your right leg to add weight to the attack. Target the solar plexus, throat or face.

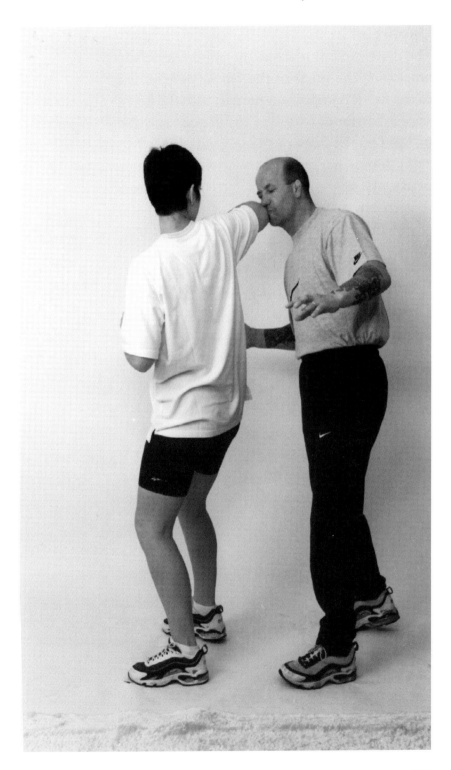

Uppercut:

The uppercut is not unlike the uppercut punch, employing the point of the elbow as opposed to the fist. It is important here to turn the body, as per illustration, into the technique. This can be used off the front or rear leg with the left or right hand, according to how you are in proximity to the target. Thrust the elbow directly upward, into and through the target. I always place the palm of the striking hand over my ear to ensure the correct technique. The uppercut, as with all elbow techniques should be flowing and relaxed as opposed to stopping at the end of the strike with rigid kime (body focus).

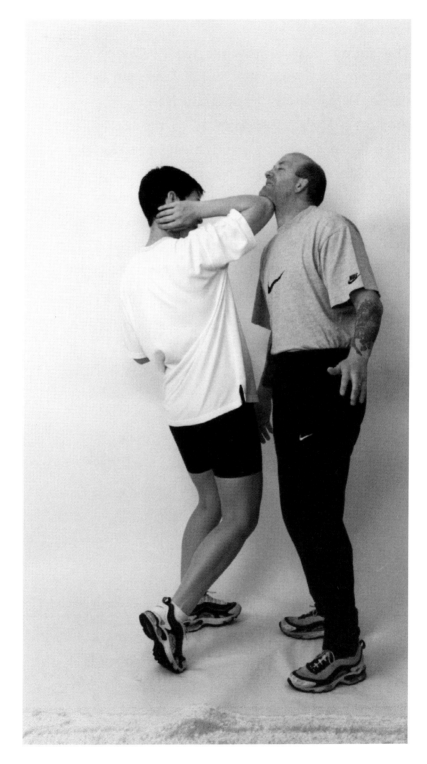

Roundhouse:

The roundhouse elbow is a lovely flowing technique from very close range. Executed in the same manner as a hook punch, using the point of the elbow as opposed to the fist to strike. Again, keep it loose and flowing, a relaxed technique it the most powerful technique. Thrown off the front or rear leg with either the right or the left hand. Throw the elbow in a circular manner (like a hook punch) directly to the target, the hand tucks in by your own chest. Be sure to drive the body weight behind the technique.

Overhand:

The overhand is really just the same as the roundhouse, only with a higher angle. This is especially useful if your opponent has a guard, you use the overhand to attack the target over the guard. The mechanics are exactly the same as the roundhouse, just a little higher with a chopping action, as per illustration, at the end of the movement.

Hacking:

The hacking elbow is specifically designed to attack the collar-bone of an opponent. Or you can aim the same technique at the face and drag it over the eyes, nose and mouth on point of impact. Bring the elbow up high above the head in a semi-circular action, as per illustration, and strike down directly at the face or collar-bone. This technique tends to come into its own if you add a jump to the beginning. As you jump use the same 'elbow above the head' action and drive down onto the target as your body weight comes back to the floor. This adds tremendous momentum to the technique. If you have an opponent on the ground you can also use the hacking elbow as a finishing strike.

Real Head, Knees & Elbows

Punching elbow:

This is a sneaky little trick, used by many of the latter day punchers who liked to add a bit of illegality to their play, and whack an opponent with the un-gloved elbow. Usually thrown off the back leg-right or left cross-but could equally be used of the front leg too. We will use the right cross as an example: throw the right cross to the opponent's head but deliberately miss and pass the side of his face, smashing him with your elbow on route, as per illustration.

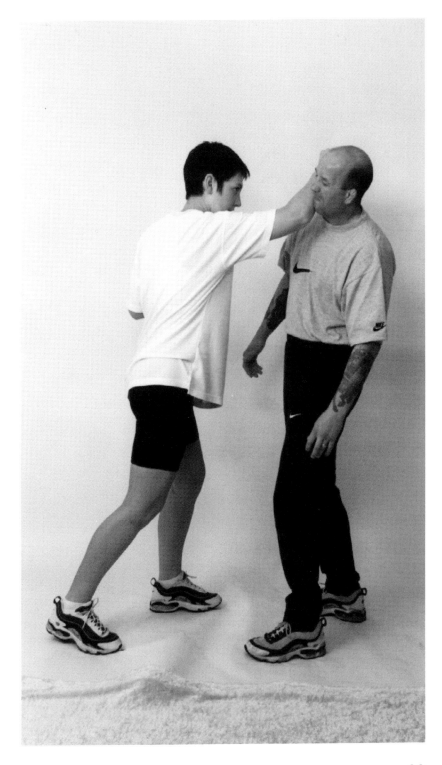

Retraction:

The retracting elbow strike is another old boxer's favourite used as a professional foul in the boxing ring. After throwing a punch that misses and goes past the head (either accidentally or deliberately to set this technique up) strike the opponent's head/ear/face with the elbow of the same arm as you retract the punch.

Drop elbow:

This is a devastating technique that destroys an opponent from the legs up. It is very similar in context to the Thai leg kick, only you are using the point of the elbow as opposed to the shin to attack. This can be used as a professional foul if you are boxing (many of the boxers choose to use the fist here as opposed to the elbow but either will suffice) or in vertical grappling range. It is a weakening technique as oppose to a finishing technique, though if delivered correctly it can also be a good finisher. What I have found though is this: even if the technique does not finish the opponent it will surely take him one step closer to the point of capitulation. There is nothing like a crack across the thigh to take the fight out of an opponent.

This is only really effective when you are close to an opponent. Drop your stance very low, as per illustration, and drive your reverse elbow-left or right depending upon which leg you lead with-into the thigh of the opponent. Try to strike with the point of the elbow. As soon as the blow has landed, return to the standing position. You could easily combine this with kneeing techniques to the thigh to take the fight out of the opponent.

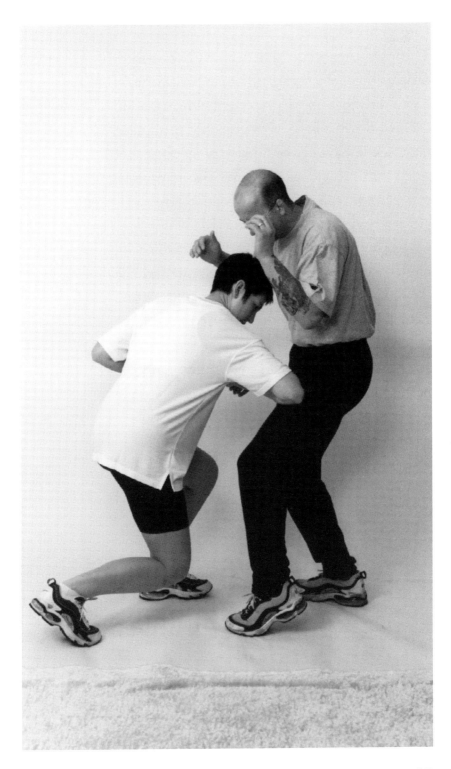

Leg grab elbow:

This is a technique that I always favoured, especially in heavy sparring and especially when I was facing a hard opponent who needed slowing down a little. It can be used from a leg catch-when you catch the kick of an opponent –or from a leg pick up – when, in vertical grappling you pick up the opponent's leg.

Once you have the leg tucked under you arm, as per illustration, smash your elbow into the thigh of the opponent, as many times as you need to ensure the right result. This can be followed by a throw, a take down or a punch – whatever presents itself to you at the time.

Angular elbows:

Angular elbows, the same as angular punches, are strikes that do not fit into the category of straight, uppercut, roundhouse strike, overhand, hacking etc. For instance you may throw an attack, to fit a specific opening in the opponent's artillery, where a conventional strike will not fit. This attack may be a cross between an uppercut and a roundhouse, or a cross between a roundhouse and overhand etc. By working this way one has an infinite number of possible strikes to choose from and no guard is without penetration. As an advance player you will probably find yourself naturally and instinctively throwing angular blows when a situation demands, whether they be with the hands, feet, elbows or whatever. It is the natural way of things to tailor all you basic and finite techniques into an ever-changing infinite artillery of combat techniques.

Conclusion

That concludes the head, knees and elbows. It also concludes the *Real Series* of books. I hope that *Real Head, Knees and Elbows* and the other texts have been of help to you the reader. Thank you very much for taking the time and the energy to read them.

I would like to say in conclusion that, although this book is predominantly about the physical aspect of self-protection – head, knees and elbows being a small part of the whole – it is not where I personally see self-protection. The physical response has to be the last resort, the ace card to pull when all else has failed. Try to avoid situation, escape them if this is not an option, use verbal dissuasion if you are cornered, only attack if there is no other option. Violence is not the answer. That is my philosophy, I hope that you might follow it. The physical response, while sometimes unavoidable, is not the answer, only undertake it if you really have to. And if you really have to then do it right, there are no half measures. Thank you again. Be a good person and karma will be kind to you.

Love and respect. God bless.

Geoff Thompson 1998